MW01124456

Letters to
the Bride

Katie Zachariou

ISBN 13 TP: 9798362136604
Cover design & artwork by: Jessica Ostrander
(jessicaoart.com)

Acknowledgements

I am extremely grateful to my husband, my kids, and my family for their love and support. You are treasures in my life. I am also thankful to Julie Brown, who provided the encouragement I needed to finish this book. Julie, you bring out the best in all the writers I know. To Jessica Ostrander, thank you for your friendship and for creating the most personally meaningful painting I've ever seen. It was the perfect cover for this book. Thank you also to my mentors and friends, Angela West and Chris Breyer, for reading and providing valuable insights during the writing process. Thank you to my editor Lisa and to Jane Gibbs, who assisted me skillfully with the publishing process. I hold each of your contributions to this work, and to my life, dear to my heart.

Foreword

Every once in a while, a book is written that touches our spirit so deeply, illuminating our pathway and opening up new realms of relationship with Jesus, that it becomes a lifetime companion, a message we never forget and will return to through all the seasons of life. 'Letters to the Bride' is such a book.

Drawing from key passages in the Song of Songs, Katie steps into the heart of Jesus to become His scribe, articulating in the most beautiful way, the multi-faceted nature of the love of the Bridegroom for His Bride.

It is as though the Spirit has taken up the pen once more, placed it in Katie's hands, expressing softly spoken words of truth to bring the Song and all its meaning home, to reside in the heart of every reader.

These letters bring Jesus very near. They are his letters to you. His voice speaks.

As you read, you will find the relentless nature of His love washing over you, breaking down barriers of doubt, fear or loneliness, reaching the very places where you need him the most.

Katie speaks as an oracle of God, revealing as the pages turn, the value not only of his love for you, but how much *your* love means to him, how he longs to fully receive this love, to enjoy a mutually enriching relationship with you, forever.

In return, if you have ever wondered *how* to love Jesus, *how* to receive or understand his love, this intimate book of letters from Jesus instructs the heart and teaches the way of intimacy in a way that is both profound and pure.

Perhaps you have found yourself saying, "Oh how I long to love Him more, but how can I love Him as He loves me?" These letters from Jesus build a magnificent bridge to lead you *out* of a winter season and *into* the summer of mature love, to a realm of experiential relationship from which you will not turn back.

'Letters to the Bride' is a lesson in love and the Bridegroom is the teacher. You will find that with each letter you read, line upon line, precept upon precept, you become convinced of the multi-faceted nature of Jesus' love for you. And you have grown. Your heart has awakened to love him in return.

In a beautiful, very sensitive way, these letters will speak right into your everyday life, where your love relationship with Jesus is truly lived out. Even in the most hidden places of quiet, sacrificial service to your family, you can hear his voice, experience his love and release the fragrance of your love to reach the heart of the King of Kings.

I love this book. Each letter is a sacred epistle from the heart of God.

I will keep it by my side through all the days of *my* journey with Jesus, knowing I will hear from him whenever I read 'Letters to the Bride.' For there he is, in the midst of every word Katie has written.

I honour and love you, Katie Zachariou.

Thank you for the high honour of writing this foreword for one of the most beautiful and meaningful books I've ever read.

Julie Brown
Author and Founder of The Proverbs 31
Movement

Contents

Introduction   15
1. An Ocean, not a Precipice   19
2. Burned but Lovely   23
3. My Fragrance   27
4. His Rose   31
5. A Lily Among Thorns   35
6. Above the Rest   39
7. From Fruitfulness to Fruitful   43
8. Proud to Be with You   51
9. Faint with Love   57
10. Gazing   61
11. Show Me Your Face   65
12 Foxes   71
13. Rise   75
14. Joy in Your Desert   81
15. True Beauty   87
16. Captivated   93
17. I Thirst   97
18. Open to Me   103
19. Night   109
20. Pierced by Love   113
21. Words Like Kisses   119
22. Transported by Longing   123
23. Beyond Compare   127
24. Taken   131

25. Wine of Love   135
26. All He Wants   139
27. Forgotten Places   145
28. The Dance   149
29. From Labor to Love   153
30. The Lord Most Passionate   159
31. The One Who Brings Him Joy   163
About the Author   167

Introduction

I believe the church is entering her finest hour. We stand upon a foundation laid by the first apostles and continued by generations of believers since. It is up to us to continue to build, both His church and our own lives, after God's heart. The way to do this is to encounter the Lord personally in the fullest way we can.

God reveals His heart to us through a variety of relational roles in the Bible— roles that he chose on purpose because he knew we would be familiar with them through our earthly experiences. As a believer of many years, I knew God as my Creator and Father. I knew Holy Spirit as my Helper, Counselor, and Comforter. I had experienced Jesus as my Savior, Lord, Healer, Deliverer, and Friend. Yet, I knew there was more. There is always more to discover about the multifaceted love of God.

On May 21, 2018, Jesus revealed another role I could begin to see Him in, the role of the Bridegroom, with me as His bride. This revelation proved to be life changing. It was as if I'd read His Word in black and white all my life, and then suddenly I saw it in vibrant color. Scriptures that had not made sense to me before, including brief verses I'd read in Song of Songs, became infinitely precious because I read them as personal love notes from my heavenly Pursuer. The truths I uncovered in the coming days were not just for me. I recorded them here for you.

It is my prayer that these thirty-one letters will take you on a month-long devotional journey that will transform you. I pray you will see Jesus, and yourself, with new eyes. I pray you will identify with the Shulamite in the Song of Songs, and that any barriers to spiritual or emotional intimacy in your heart will be resolved. From now on, may you see yourself as the focus of Jesus' tender affection and fierce devotion.

May you see yourself as His beloved, His chosen, His *bride*.

An Ocean, not a Precipice

Take me with you, and we'll run away; be my
king and take me to your room.
We will be happy together, drink deep, and lose
ourselves in love.
~ Song of Songs 1:4 GNT

My love is a bottomless ocean you may swim in, not a precipice you must stand on. The idea that you must precariously balance upon life to keep from falling out of my affection does not come from me. I invite you further into the depths of love. I do not *breed fear* by telling you that you may somehow miss it.

No, there is no missing my all-consuming love once your eyes are opened to it. If I led you to the beach, would you miss the ocean? How could you? For you would see it stretch seemingly endless before you. It would be impossible to miss.

My love is so vast you can get lost in it, beloved. You can lose yourself and your own ambitions, you can lose your disappointments and your fears. The sweetness and happiness to be found in me drowns out guilt and regret.

My delight in you is not narrow. I will not constrict you into a tiny mold of perfection, but I will coax the personality I've placed within you into its full, sanctified expression. I will show you how to be the freest you that you can be.

The room of acceptance that I invite you into is altogether different than what you are accustomed to on earth. A gentleness is in this room, an embrace so expansive, so sweeping, it is like a panoramic hug. There is limitless room to stretch, run, dance, explore, and grow here. There is room to play, believe, and rejoice without suddenly slipping out of favor. There is room to learn.

Allow yourself to acclimate to the warm-hearted temperature of grace.

For my love is all-embracing. The sun does not warm the earth subjectively, rationing out rays to portions it deems deserving. It bathes the entire planet with warmth that radiates from its core. So I bathe you in delight that exudes from the core of who I am.

Take time to journal your heart's response:

_____

_____

_____

_____

_____

_____

_____

_____

_____

_____

_____

_____

_____

_____

_____

_____

_____

_____

_____

_____

_____

_____

Burned but Lovely

I am deeply tanned but lovely, O daughters of
Jerusalem,
[I am dark] like the tents of [the Bedouins of]
Kedar,
Like the [beautiful] curtains of Solomon.
Do not gaze at me because I am deeply tanned,
[I have worked in] the sun; it has left its mark
on me.
My mother's sons were angry with me;
They made me keeper of the vineyards,
But my own vineyard (my complexion) I have
not kept.
~ Song of Songs 1:5–6 AMP

During busy seasons of life, your flower
does not fade, *your loveliness grows.*

Your desire to tend and steward all I put into
your care is breathtaking, for unselfishly nurt-
uring others, managing resources, and
tending to responsibilities is a mark of my
character. But hear me call you even higher,
away from a place of lonely work to a life

union. A partnership. A life of love-reliance on me.

In this high calling, I infuse my strength into you. There, it is no longer you who lives, works, and bears burdens. *It is me.* It is Christ in you, your hope of glory. (See Colossians 1:27)

To step into this calling, first realize your responsibilities are never yours alone. This life is a relay race, and we are in it together. Every baton (burden) that falls into your hands must go through my hands first. Once a baton (burden) comes to you, remember to quickly pass it back to me.

Do not pause to contemplate the weight or significance of the baton. Do not wonder how it will affect your life. The simple act of surrender in passing each earthly care to me in prayer shows we are one. It is a testimony of our unified relationship. Your trust is recognized in heaven. As Romans 4:5 says, "To the one who does not work but trusts

God who justifies the ungodly, their faith is credited as righteousness."

Each time you pass a burden (baton) to me, righteousness is credited to your heavenly account. In this way, earthly cares only cause your heavenly credits to grow.

Remember that your reliance on me is never a chore or annoyance. My involvement in your daily life is evidence of our covenant. My shoulders are broad, and my strength unending. The batons you hand me are lighter than dust.

Take time to journal your heart's response:

_____

_____

_____

_____

_____

_____

_____

_____

_____

_____

_____

_____

_____

_____

_____

_____

_____

_____

_____

_____

My Fragrance

When my King-Lover lay down beside me,
my fragrance filled the room.
~ Song of Solomon 1:12 MSG

Do you know you are reading this because I have made the first move toward intimacy with you?

I have drawn you through mysterious means at times, which you may not have noticed at first glance. An inspiring word from a friend. A song on the radio. A sunrise that sets your mind on my creation. A sudden desire to hear from me. I have initiated many things with the purpose of bringing you into an awareness of my nearness.

The love-soaked verses you read in my letters all point to my deep desire for you. I have come very close to you now. I have even laid down beside your heart, for you are my chosen resting place. I want to hear what is important to you.

I am nearer than your breath, for in me, you live, move, and have your being. And my nearness has elicited a response from you. Oh, you may not notice it, but I have. I can smell it in the atmosphere. It is the fragrance of love being awakened.

When Mary broke her jar of precious ointment and anointed my feet in Bethany, a fragrance filled that room too. The religious leaders missed its value. They belittled, accused, and criticized her. They mocked her extravagance, but I—oh, all I could think of was her love. I breathed it in with great joy and created an everlasting memorial to it in my WORD.

Her love wrapped my heart before the hardness of Golgotha. It encapsulated me and prepared me for burial. It surrounded me, body and spirit, and I want to do the same for you. I want to insulate you by wrapping you in the thrill of being wanted.

In the joy of being celebrated. In the security of being cherished by me always.

Do you see my love covering you like a cloak today? If you do, you will walk through life with confidence and a settled heart that has its most vital question already answered. You will know you are wanted. You will know I am with you—and even beyond that, you will know we are one. We are wrapped in unending love and light, two as one for eternity.

Allow me to comfort and shield you from the hardness of earthly things. Let the truth of my desire for you anoint and run over your being as healing oil. For I am here now, and your fragrance—the fragrance of love being awakened—has already filled the room.

Take time to journal your heart's response:

_____

_____

_____

_____

_____

_____

_____

_____

_____

_____

_____

_____

_____

_____

_____

_____

_____

_____

His Rose

I am truly his rose, the very theme of his song.
I'm overshadowed by his love,
like a lily growing in the valley!
~ Song of Songs 2:1 TPT

In the same way you would buy a bouquet—
not because you need it but because you
want it—and then place it in the central part
of your home to admire its beauty, so my
admiration is focused on you. See yourself
as the focus of my admiration, my rose.

Great artists and composers have subjects
that inspire them. Lyricists find pleasure in
observing objects of interest. Then they turn
their observations into harmonies, melodies,
and symphonies. Without an object of delight
and observation, without a focus, there can
be no inspiration.

You are my inspiration and my focus and
not merely a temporary fascination. You are

not a fleeting fancy, an object used to churn out another song in a heavenly playlist only to be tossed out after production ceases.

No, never. You are not generic stock music.

You exude life, variation, and value. You are intrinsically unique, the continual center of heavenly interest and activity. You are like a beehive when the bees buzz about it with great delight. You are the apple of my eye.

You are the theme song of my heart. Warm words and feelings about you spill out of me and form with ease into musical expressions of love. Oh yes, I sing over you. (See Zephaniah 3:17.) I gain a continual stream of inspiration from observing you.

I have shown your value by placing you, my rose, in a protected place. You have not been planted beside a thoroughfare where you may be trampled. You have not been left in a desert where you would dry up and shrivel. You have been lovingly planted in the valley of my own heart, tucked into my side, where

blood and water flowed out during my crucifixion. See yourself in my side today,
beloved, where you are kept infinitely close
and safe.

Take time to journal your heart's response:

_____

_____

_____

_____

_____

_____

_____

_____

_____

_____

_____

_____

_____

_____

_____

A Lily Among Thorns

Like a lily among thorns is my darling among
the young women.
~ Song of Songs 2:2 NIV

Some days, you may feel unworthy of my
love. Your perceived shortcomings seem like
glaring red stop signs, declaring your lack of
fitness to walk closely with me. The enemy
takes the signposts you erect and posts them
at the twists and turns of your life. He taunts
you with them, declaring your faults are
causes for my judgement, causes for a chasm
of distance and separation between us. But he
lies. And his attempts to bind a banner of
unworthiness over your heart will fail.

There now, come to me.

See yourself correctly. Hear me call you my
lily—bright, clean, beautiful, and completely

lovely—among thorns. Renew your mind by understanding my view, which is truth.

I do not compare you to other saints and wish you were like them. I do not wish you had another's gifts or qualities. I have created you uniquely special and precious. When you call to me, I recognize the distinctive tempo of your voice. I rejoice in what makes you different. I thrill at the exclusive cadence of your heartbeat.

I am your sufficiency. I, your Good Shepherd, delight to lead you in my ways. Yes, I am intimately acquainted with the thorns in your life. I know each cruel word, each bitter discouragement, and each harsh circumstance that seeks to steal your attention. But put your eyes on me, beloved. Because *my eyes are settled on you*. Come very near to me now.

Yes, I want you here—right next to me. Right beside me on my throne, beloved, where you will hear my heartbeat. Hearing my heartbeat with love for you will cause my tender affection to seep into your whole being.

Let me speak kindly to you now. Let me hear your voice. Tell me what concerns you.

Do you hear me answering you, addressing you as my lily? As a flower among brambles, you are rare and precious to me. You are *wanted*. I desire to hold you in my hands and set you on a table in my house where I may admire your beauty.

Look to me, radiant one. Your spirit is glowing brightly with my glory. My sacrifice, even my crown of thorns, has transformed you into a crown of pure treasure. I took the piercings of life for you. The cruelty of sin sank into my flesh because of the *great* longing I have for you—the longing that brought you near when you were very far away. So toss every sign of shame behind you and *run to me*.

I will always embrace you.

Take time to journal your heart's response:

_____

_____

_____

_____

_____

_____

_____

_____

_____

_____

_____

_____

_____

_____

_____

_____

_____

_____

Above the Rest

My beloved is to me the most fragrant apple
tree—he stands above the sons of men.
~ Song of Songs 2:3 TPT

He alone is my beloved. He shines in dazzling
splendor yet is still so approachable—without
equal as he stands above all others,
outstanding among ten thousands!
~ Song of Songs 5:10 TPT

Do you realize you live among reflections,
beloved? Yes, you spend your days among
glimpses of my image. But I desire you to
recognize me as your pure source. For as an
image is projected from its origin, so the
admirable things you witness in people are
projected from my heart of love toward you.
But there is more. I desire you to come
further still and witness even more. I desire
you to drink from the primary source.

Parched travelers would not stop and
permanently camp at a trickle of water. They

would seek the original wellspring. Enjoy the gifts in others, but then continue your journey. Follow the signs of my presence onward to yet deeper places in me. Come forward and experience overflow, as David did when he said, "You give me all I can drink of you until my cup overflows" (Psalm 23:5).

Overflow in me looks like excessive peace. It feels like a flood of joy beyond what is needed or imagined. It manifests as a super-abundance of love that surprises and over-whelms you.

Rather than fighting, forcing, or struggling, overflow will become the force that carries you through life. Just as a powerful current picks up tree branches and rushes them downriver, so I desire to pick you up and shuttle you onward to new places in me.

Will you let go of all that seeks to entangle you? Will you release everything into my hands? Simply cease from grasping and trust me to transport you to new destinations in me.

Take time to journal your heart's response:

_____

_____

_____

_____

_____

_____

_____

_____

_____

_____

_____

_____

_____

_____

_____

_____

From Fruitless to Fruitful

My beloved is to me
the most fragrant apple tree—
he stands above the sons of men.
Sitting under his grace-shadow,
I blossom in his shade,
enjoying the sweet taste of his pleasant,
delicious fruit,
resting with delight where his glory never
fades.
Song of Solomon 2:3–4 TPT

In my Word, people are often referred to as trees. This symbolism is repeated many times because it communicates so much.

Trees hold the soil in place and prevent it from sliding. They provide nesting places for birds as well as food and recreation for creatures that climb. Trees cleanse the air of impurities. They make food by drawing on the power of the sun.

Aside from these attributes, I want you to focus on one component: fruit. Some trees bear fruit while others do not.

Within humanity, you meet many resourceful people. I've planted gifts in the hearts of men and women, and these gifts can be mesmerizing. But there is a difference between gifts and fruit. Among the human race, I stand tall in a way that no other can. I offer lasting fruit like no other can.

I invite you to come closer, to sit and simply rest beneath my shade. I want to comfort you. I want to enjoy you. And I want *you* to enjoy *me*. Do you know when you enjoy me, the pleasure I feel motivates me to provide the very desires of your deepest heart? Yes, your enjoyment of my presence compels me to do even *more* for you. (See Psalm 37:4.)

This is the fellowship I desire, not a communion based on rehearsing faults and demands but fellowship based on mutual enjoyment. The very first environment where I placed man was called Eden, or "place of pleasure."

So if you feel rejected by others, peer inside my branches. Find the friendship you long for. Are you troubled? Come closer until you taste my peace. Are you full of doubts about the future? Nothing can harm you in my shadow. I will shield you from the world's harsh rays. Not only that, but I will take that harmful radiation and transform it into food that makes you *strong*.

Yes, beloved, I desire to make you strong and stronger still. You are a warrior bride who will not buckle under a fight—because *I am with you to sustain you.*

The world attempts to sell its own fruit in glossy media campaigns. It dangles status, appearance, position, material possessions, and new relationships. But it offers fake fruit. Outward solutions cannot satisfy a heart that beats with a need for me. Those imposter fruits fade. Their temporary joy disintegrates before reaching the deepest part of mankind, the spirit.

The deep parts of me call to the deep parts of you.

I am not afraid of commitment—I seek it. I am not afraid of vulnerability—I require it. My love wants complete access to your life. Will you completely abandon yourself to me?

Do you trust me to know what season you are in? Do you believe I will offer the appropriate fruit for each specific season?

I don't offer more relationships when what you really need is to know the depths of my loyalty. I don't offer material things when what you really need is deep-rooted peace. I don't offer a renewed outward appearance when what you really need is to know my all-consuming fascination with you—exactly as you are.

Being near each other is worth the effort our love relationship requires. Every distance I've crossed, every pain I've endured, pales in comparison to the great joy of knowing you intimately.

When we enjoy each other in prayer, when heaven and earth join hands in us, both realms stop to celebrate the union. The angels loudly rejoice. And I *revel* in our fellowship. I don't passively celebrate, dear bride. I rejoice wildly over you. I dance and sing. I drink in the joy of our union, then offer this exhilarating wine to you.

Will you take this cup?

This wine is the highest currency of heaven. It was created when I was crushed for you, when I was trampled under men's feet because I wanted you to arise. I promise to love you always and hold you close.

Will you take this cup?

It is my own blood, drained from my body for you. It is evidence of your worth, dear bride. I willingly laid my all down for you.

My eyes are on you now. Are your eyes on me? Do you see my fruit hanging low from the branches? I don't place what you need out of your reach. I put it near enough to touch your face and brush your cheek. Communion with me is accessed where I dwell, within your very own heart.

I am not a universe away, beloved. I am not in a vague, unknown location that you must access from many dimensions away. I am not even a church service away. I am close enough that you can smell, desire, and taste the sweetness of our fellowship. I am within you.

Taste and see. My love isn't picky, self-centered, and vain. My love isn't stand-offish. No, never. It is infinitely intimate. Closer than air. Deeper than sea. Stronger than any binding worldly agreement.

My love holds the universe together, and it is focused on you.

Take time to journal your heart's response:

_____

_____

_____

_____

_____

_____

_____

_____

_____

_____

_____

_____

_____

_____

_____

_____

_____

_____

Proud to Be With You

He escorts me to the banquet hall;
it's obvious how much he loves me.
~ Song of Solomon 2:4 NLT

He brought me to the wine chamber and placed
his banner of love over me.
~ Song of Solomon 2:4 Jubilee Bible 2000

Do you know friends or loved ones who make you wonder where you stand with them? On some days, you feel valued; on other days, you are unsure about your place in their heart. Or have you ever felt small in someone's presence, as if they may not want to be seen with you?

You will not ever find yourself in those places with me. I leave no room for guesses about my love for you.

Before the planets were hung in space, before Adam committed the first sin, *before you were born*, I made my intentions clear: I claimed you for my own. "I am the Lamb who was slain from the creation of the world" (Revelation 13:8 NIV).

When I foresaw the separation brought into humanity by sin, when I peeked through the portal of time and glimpsed you struggling alone through your life and going alone to your grave, I didn't waste time pondering what to do about you. I didn't mull over my options while earth drifted into chaos.

I spoke up for you *before* you needed me. Before you felt the sting of helplessness, I offered all I had for you. Because I longed to be with you forever.

"When we were utterly helpless, with no way of escape, Christ came at just the right time and died for us sinners who had no use for him. Even if we were good, we really wouldn't expect anyone to die for us. But *God showed his great love* for us by sending

Christ to die for us while we were still sinners." (Romans 5:6–8 TLB, emphasis added)

My love does not play games, beloved. I do not keep my intentions mysterious or make you beg for affirmation. It is not my glory to withhold attention from you. My ways are high above worldly ways. (See Isaiah 55:9) I willingly made a spectacle of my love for you.

On Calvary, I lifted myself like a banner and announced to all of heaven that you had conquered my heart. I rejoiced then and rejoice now when all the world sees that we share an eternal bond, that we have chosen each other, and our covenant will outlast time itself.

I desire to show you off.

When earthly couples admire each other, they may doodle one another's names in diaries. Or they may etch their love into a tree. Beloved, I have written our love story in the stars. I have recorded it in the heavens forever. Your name is carved into my very hands, my feet, and my side.

I have marked you with my love.

When earthly couples enter into union, they exchange a ring. They are excited to show off their relationship, to show they belong to their beloved. I have sealed you with my presence as a mark of my overwhelming affection for you. This presence-seal serves as an announcement to every saint and angel. It declares I'm excited about you. I am thrilled that you call me your beloved!

"Who has placed his mark of ownership upon us, and who has given us the Holy Spirit in our hearts as the guarantee of all that he has in store for us"* (2 Corinthians 1:22 GNT, emphasis added).

Your presence gives me joy. So let me lavish my joy on you. You are my crown, and I delight to see you shine.

Look at each sunrise, meadow, flower, mountain, stream—look at everything lovely—but don't just *look*. Ask me to help you *perceive*. I want to adjust your spiritual sight. I want to fine-tune your perception so you will notice my *obvious,* visible, intentional, and tangible love that surrounds you.

Take time to journal your heart's response:

_____

_____

_____

_____

_____

_____

_____

_____

_____

_____

_____

_____

Faint With Love

Oh! Give me something refreshing to eat—and
quickly! Apricots, raisins—anything. I'm about
to faint with love! His left hand cradles my
head, and his right arm encircles my waist!
~ Song of Solomon 2:5–6 MSG

Do you feel faint, my love?

Do your knees buckle in my presence? Like
my disciples on the Road to Emmaus, does
your heart burn within you for more time
with me? Or has your inner man grown dull
of sight and hearing?

If it has, simply turn toward me.

Allow me to embrace you. Let the power of
my love exhilarate you. It will not leave you
spent, bruised, abused, abandoned, or rejected. My love is completely unique.

It is fierce in loyalty but gentle in expression. I will not knock you down to make you fall for me. No, I will gently sweep you off your feet with sweetness.

If you are tired, see my left hand cradle your head. Like a parent hovering over a small child, you are the center of my watchful care. I will comfort you when you cry out and hold you, safe and secure.

Do you need strength?

See my arm encircle your waist. I don't bend to condescend if you stumble. I don't look down my nose and lecture. No. I wrap my arm around you like your beloved, wanting to turn your head.

Will you allow me to turn your attention now? Away from distractions, temporary needs, and even your own shortcomings? There now, look to me.

Hear me whisper words of love like an adoring groom into his bride's ear. I see such growth in you, such beauty to adore. Beneath the surface of your heart, seeds of love and tenderness are sprouting. My love is calling to your love.

We belong together.

Let me hold you here. I know you have desires and needs. I understand and care for them all. But in this moment, do you hear me saying, "Only one thing is needful?"

Lock eyes with me. Don't rush from this moment, from this embrace. There is warmth here and healing. There is fullness of joy for those who will linger.

Take time to journal your heart's response:

_____

_____

_____

_____

_____

_____

_____

_____

_____

_____

_____

_____

_____

_____

_____

_____

_____

_____

_____

Gazing

Now he comes closer, even to the places where
I hide. He gazes into my soul, peering through
the portal as he blossoms within my heart ...
The one I love calls to me: Arise, my dearest.
Hurry, my darling. Come away with me! I have
come as you have asked to draw you to my
heart and lead you out. For now is the time, my
beautiful one. The season has changed, the
bondage of your barren winter has ended, and
the season of hiding is over and gone.
~ Song of Songs 2:9–11 TPT

Have you ever found yourself staring at
something while caught in a lovely day-
dream? The object you focused on was so
inspiring that it transported you to another
time or place, another memory. Many parents
do this. They find themselves randomly
staring at their child, simply because they
are fascinating.

Any curiosity you have experienced is a fraction
of the deep interest I have in you.

I see you when you feel life has backed you into a corner of fear. I see you looking for answers. I see you wondering where I am. I am here, my bride. I am gazing into your soul with love.

Can you see me now, looking on you with supreme interest and care, not condemnation? I wait to show mercy to you, to lift you on wings of faith. To draw you to the security of my heart and lead you out. The season of doing everything on your own is over. I long to lead you through life. Take my hand and we will navigate all things together.

Take time to journal your heart's response:

_____

_____

_____

_____

_____

_____

_____

_____

_____

_____

_____

_____

_____

_____

_____

_____

_____

_____

Show Me Your Face

My dove in the clefts of the rock, in the hiding
places on the mountainside, show me your
face, let me hear your voice; for your voice is
sweet, and your face is lovely.
~ Song of Solomon 2:14 NIV

It is wise to hide under certain circumstances.
Throughout history, people have hidden
from tyrannical leaders who were bent on
destroying them. Once, young David hid in
a field (1 Samuel 20:5–4). He also hid in a
cave from the tyrant King Saul had become
(1 Samuel 24:3). Young Moses's mother hid
him in a basket among the bulrushes from a
Pharaoh who raged against innocent babies
(Exodus 2:2–3). My father hid me, too, from
Herod, who was consumed with killing the
King of the Jews (Matthew 2:13–14).

These choices to hide were necessary. The
leaders in these stories had violent intentions

and the means to carry them out. But sometimes the choice to hide is unnecessary. Not only unnecessary but counterproductive.

As with Adam and Eve.

They hid because of shame (Genesis 3:8–10). Disappointment in themselves and their choices led them to believe something about me that wasn't true. They thought I would destroy them. But my heart is to restore and redeem.

Earthly rulers may be driven by selfish ambition, but I was driven by a love so great it possessed me to give everything. A love so great, I would rather die than be separated. Do you ever meditate on that, beloved? That I chose to die rather than be separated from you? Do you realize that I wasn't able to bear the thought of our being apart?

Adam and Eve were bitten and injected with poison from the accusing snake. But sadly, they didn't realize I possessed the antivenom. One dose of my love and acceptance could've cleared away his venom of accusation and shame.

So if the snake bites or lies to you, remember the truth. If he says I will reject, I will receive. If he says I will destroy, I will heal. If he says to hide from me, run straight into my open arms. Think of the most sought-after views on earth. The grandest beauties people travel to, the ones they marvel at through telescope lenses. The Eiffel Tower, tropical islands, waterfalls, galaxies—your face captivates me more than those. The earth and stars will grow old and wear out like a garment, but I have given you eternal life with me.

Your face delights me, so don't hide it. Come and appear before me in prayer. Think of your favorite song on earth. If someone purchased a front-row seat to that artist's concert, would you miss it? Your voice thrills me more than that.

So don't stay quiet. Come boldly out in the open where I can welcome you.

I want to expose the snake's lies that say I won't receive you. Because there isn't a part of you I don't long for. Your wounds, disappointments, and mistakes do not hinder my love. When you are hurt or broken, I seek you all the more. I am not put off by the parts of your heart that you wish were different.

Listen to my voice say: "I made you who you are on purpose." I am calling you near to me now. Can you hear me asking where you are? Although I know your location, I want to see if you desire my love like I desire yours.

Today is the day. Now is the hour. This is the time of your visitation. Let me surround you with the acceptance you've been seeking all your life. Nothing in heaven, earth, or even under the earth can keep my love from you.

I am attending a concert of the sound of your voice. I marvel at your beauty, the appearance of your face. My love seeks you in every hiding place of discouragement and brightens the darkness of fear and shame. My seeking love did not come just for others as the snake would have you believe. It came for *you*. For you, for you, for you. I have come for you. Let those words become your anthem, the love song you hear me singing over your life.

Take time to journal your heart's response:

_____

_____

_____

_____

_____

_____

_____

_____

_____

_____

_____

_____

Foxes

You must catch the troubling foxes, those sly little foxes that hinder our relationship. For they raid our budding vineyard of love to ruin what I've planted within you. Will you catch them and remove them for me? We will do it together.
~ Song of Songs 2:15 TPT

Jesus told them, "Go and tell that deceiver [fox] *that I will continue to cast out demons and heal the sick today and tomorrow, and on the third day I will bring my work to perfection."*
~ Luke 13:32 TPT, emphasis and word added

Mary sought my body at the garden tomb. But when she encountered me alive, she mistook me for the gardener. This was not an accident. It is a picture of my work in your life, which is like that of a gardener. I plant you and care for you tenderly. I nourish you with warmth and feed your inner man with my presence. I send the rain of my Spirit to awaken you to my love. Then I watch as your own love for me grows.

But how long can love burn brightly when cold water is poured upon it?

That is what the enemy seeks to do to your love for me, beloved. He uses deception and doubts about my faithful nature to injure your devotion. He does this subtly, through twisting your experiences and thoughts, attempting to deceive you into believing I will somehow leave or fail you.

The enemy, like Herod from my day, is a fox. He is inferior to the lion that lives within you, so he must hide. He disguises himself among the landscape of your life experiences and presents you a false interpretation of them. He will never acknowledge my love and devotion to you. Instead, he places a negative slant on all the circumstances you face so that you doubt who I am. By hiding and feeding you with false input, he seeks to undermine our relationship.

Since he hides, he must be caught. You can do this by keeping watch over the thoughts that enter your heart. If they cause you to doubt the power of my love, hold them under the light of my Word. By doing so, you will see their true source.

The fox not only hides himself, he wants to cause you to hide too. Do you remember that Adam and Eve hid from me in the garden? They had never done so before. But the entrance of fear causes this reaction.

The solution to fear is my love. With love, I call you out into the open. With love, I draw you with cords of kindness. (See Jeremiah 31:3) With love, I call those things that are not as though they are. (See Romans 4:17) With love, I announce to you where we will go and what we will do, *together*.

"Together" is a word that expresses faith in my love. "Alone" is a word that expresses the belief that my love will fail you. I have never called you to be solitary. Did I not say I would not leave you as an orphan? (See

John 14:18) I will never leave you helpless or alone.

Come, and let us remove each slyly twisted thought, every hidden fox of fear, together.

Take time to journal your heart's response:

_____

_____

_____

_____

_____

_____

_____

_____

_____

_____

_____

_____

_____

Rise

Why did I let him go from me? How my heart
now aches for him, but he is nowhere to be
found! So I must rise in search of him, looking
throughout the city, seeking until I find him.
Even if I have to roam through every street,
nothing will keep me from my search.
~ Song of Songs 3:1–2 TPT

The pages of Scripture are a record of journeys filled with the details of men and women seeking. Some embarked on holy searches, and some did not. Adam craved knowledge. Cain desired dominance. Abraham sought a homeland. Moses journeyed for freedom. The children of Israel wanted meat. Then they desired a king. Ruth wanted protection. Esther sought deliverance. David yearned for a temple. Herod hunted the King of the Jews. The Jews looked for a Messiah.

But you, dear bride, already belong to me, and you are being led on an internal journey. This journey will prepare you for my ultimate return. It is a journey into your own heart where I seek to enjoy my union with you.

Every search includes obstacles. Natural journeys include natural obstacles, such as mountains, deserts, or rivers. Throughout Scripture, I led my people through those obstacles to show you it can be done within your own heart as well.

When you feel a mountain of separation between us, do not be distressed. This is only an invitation to journey with greater focus. I will help you develop deep devotion to traverse it. When you encounter a wilderness season, do not fear drought or lack. I will sustain you by giving more of myself, your manna from heaven. When you face a river, a circumstance that seemingly cannot be crossed, take comfort that I will do miracles for you.

But you must rise.

You must move from a lower position to a higher position in your heart. How do you do this? First, consider what occupies the lower places. The lower places of the heart are places surrounding earthly things and thoughts.

Being lower does not indicate unimportance. All the issues of your life are vitally important to me. I do not overlook one thing that pertains to your well-being. However, these are secondary to heavenly things because they do not last.

Everything natural was birthed from the supernatural. Earthly things are like shadows. They are byproducts of heavenly things. Those who desire to eat well on earth will locate a healthy source of food, a wholesome farm. So it is the same. If it is health of the heart you seek, remember that your heart is created for eternal life with me. So come to me as the eternal origin of peace and wholeness.

And this is not difficult. It is a very gentle process. Did I not say I have already placed eternity in your heart? (See Ecclesiastes 3:11.) Yes, your own heart is where the search begins. It is the gateway to heavenly things.

By meditating on me and our heavenly home, you will subtly start to untangle from earthly weights and rise internally. Just as a balloon that is released from its string, you will swell with peace and soar upward in your heart. You will ascend into the high places. You will experience eternal places of companionship and communion with me.

Take time to journal your heart's response:

_____

_____

_____

_____

_____

_____

_____

_____

_____

_____

_____

_____

_____

_____

_____

_____

_____

_____

_____

_____

Joy in Your Desert

Who is this sweeping in from the wilderness
like a cloud of smoke?
Who is it, fragrant with myrrh and
frankincense
and every kind of spice? Look, it is Solomon's
carriage,
surrounded by sixty heroic men,
the best of Israel's soldiers. They are all skilled
swordsmen,
experienced warriors.
Each wears a sword on his thigh,
ready to defend the king against an attack in
the night.
~ Song of Solomon 3:6–8 NLT

When you find yourself in a desert season, beloved, I do not leave you to wilt. I do not want the sun's harsh rays to wither your delicate petals. But like the Shulamite, you must look for me. You must *notice* me.

For I can be missed.

The enemy creates desert illusions. Through fear, he attempts to make your present circumstances loom so large, you miss my entrance. But recognize his tricks. The ideas that I have left you helpless, directionless, and purposeless do *not* come from me. Indeed, the thought that I would ever leave my chosen bride to wander through her life like a nomad in the wilderness is unthinkable. Do not lend your ears to such beliefs.

Instead, open your ears and eyes *to me*. Do you see me rising on the sandy horizon of your life like a pillar of fire and smoke? A sight so grand and glorious, you are tempted to believe it is a desert mirage?

Keep looking. As your gaze trains on me, I will come into focus. And you will see I am no mirage. I am real, I am *here*, and I am coming for you, my beloved. As the very name Solomon means peace, so my carriage of peace comes for you, to sweep you away, releasing you from every earthly entanglement.

My angelic attendants and carriage gleam against the dust of your life like a sight from another world, because *I am* from another world—the world you share with me. Yes, your heavenly home has sent a caravan to retrieve you.

Do you remember what I told you? Your heavenly home never lacks any good thing. And you are a citizen there. So you are never left helpless—no, not *ever*.

Now that I've drawn closer, do you see my face? My mouth does not draw down at the corners. There is no hint of displeasure in my countenance. I am smiling. I am laughing. I am shouting. I am leaping from my seat to dance for joy! For I am not here on some menial errand. I have not come to collect stones in this wilderness. I have come to collect *my bride*. My chosen wife! This is the day of *my bliss*.

My heart overflows its banks with joy. Do you see it? Joy is spilling out of me and running into *you*. Rivers of life, rivers of joy are flowing to you.

My joyful presence in your inner man makes you strong in spite of any circumstance. My life flows through your veins. My can-do power covers your discouragement and despair, turning them into hopeful courage. Take my hand. Enter my carriage of peace. Together, this wasteland will become our wonderland.

Take time to journal your heart's response:

_____

_____

_____

_____

_____

_____

_____

_____

_____

_____

_____

_____

_____

_____

_____

_____

_____

_____

True Beauty

My darling, everything about you is beautiful, and there is nothing at all wrong with you [you have no blemish].
~ Song of Solomon 4:7 Expanded Bible

Let these words sink in, beloved. Let them soak into the deepest parts of your being, removing the stain of guilt and shame. Let them buff away the tarnish of earth's atmosphere.

Since the fall of man, earthly minds have been skewed. They no longer discern beauty and worth correctly. Earthly language is filled with so many words of lack: almost, barely enough, could've been, and should've been.

Earthly minds are shrouded by blemished thinking and deficits. Do not let this thinking rule you. When words of insufficiency are spoken over you, beloved, I call them lies.

You were created for better things. You were created for heavenly realities. Heavenly language has no regret. We keep no record of wrongs. There is no talk of deficit or threat of lack.

I created you as I created Eve for Adam. She was made to be a helper, a companion suited to her beloved's work and desires. You are *my* companion. You are perfectly designed to accompany me in my work and desires. You are not deadweight, dear bride. When I think of you, not a single regret enters my mind. I'm not *almost* satisfied with you.

I am fully delighted by you.

Having you by my side thrills me. Having you beside me completes the Father's design. Do you hear his voice echoing down through the ages, declaring about our oneness, "It is good, it is good, it is *very good*"?

Do you hear his satisfaction with you as well as mine?

We are united in our love for you, dear one, as Father, Spirit, and Son. Our bond is a powerful, unbreakable union. I have pulled you into this love through the cross. I have seated you with me in heaven. Do you know that's where you exist at this very moment?

You have been granted dual citizenship. Although you are present on earth, you are also simultaneously seated in heavenly places with me. (See Ephesians 2:6) You are seated securely in my righteousness and affection.

As Adam and Eve walked, talked, and stewarded life together in the garden of Eden, so we steward your life together now. So drink deeply of this truth today. Do you see me walking with you? Do you see me sharing this day with you?

Yes, drink deep of this reality. Hear me say you are a bride who captivates my heart with her beauty. A bride who fills me with joy and anticipation. A bride who is suited to me in every way as Eve was created especially for Adam. You are a joy and a song to me.

We are meant for this, you and I. We are meant for the work set before us. We are meant for the race set before us. We are meant for the love between us.

Whatever we face, we face together. My Spirit energizes you now with power to meet every demand that weighs heavy on you. Hear me say to lack and blemish-minded thinking, 'Be gone!' There is nothing—nothing, ever—that you will face without me.

Our love, friendship, and oneness know no end. There is no height, depth, length, width, no trouble or principality; there is nothing in all creation that can divorce you from my love. (Romans 8:38-39) What God has joined together can never be separated.

Take time to journal your heart's response:

_____

_____

_____

_____

_____

_____

_____

_____

_____

_____

_____

_____

_____

_____

_____

_____

_____

_____

Captivated

You've captured my heart, dear friend. You
looked at me, and I fell in love. One look my
way and I was hopelessly in love! How
beautiful your love, dear, dear friend—
far more pleasing than a fine, rare wine.
Song of Solomon 4:9–10 MSG

Can you identify the top five things that
make you happy? How about the top three?
The top one?

Many who are called by my name are not
aware that I take delight in certain things
too. I revel in happiness, just as they do. My
children are made in my image, and they
reflect my nature in more ways than they
realize. Just as you are thrilled and enthralled
by your favorite things, I am too.

So I ask, do you know what makes me happy?

Many throughout time have assumed I desired
minimal interaction with mankind. Perhaps

they've thought I only wanted servitude, mere employees in a cosmic organization.

Those views are unthinkable for many reasons but especially because they reduce the love I have for you to an earthly idea of relationship.

I do not need employees. Or mere servants. Or objects for occasional interaction. Why would I give my life to obtain any of those things?

I gave my life because I love you and not just with a casual love. When I saw through the tunnel of eternity that you would one day cast a look in my direction, I fell deeply in love with you.

I anticipated the moment you would turn to me with every breath you took. I passed time by numbering your days, the hairs on your head, and by dreaming up good works and imagining the day that you would walk in them. I planned for your fulfillment, your peace, your future, and the joy of our union.

I looked forward to the day you would be called by my name.

Remember, it was said I endured the cross "for the joy set before me"? You were the joy set before me. I endured as Jacob endured for Rachel. He indentured himself to Laban for fourteen years of service, and those years seemed to him as only one day. Every obstacle that blocked Jacob from union with Rachel was overcome with joy because she had ravished his heart.

Being with her was its own reward.

When our hearts beat with common purpose, intent, and communion, I, too, am enraptured with delight. Turning inward and considering me in your daily life makes my heart thrill with joy.

You possess the ability to capture my heart all over again, every day, by merely glancing my way. When you pick up my letters, when you raise your voice in prayer, when you lift your thoughts heavenward to me, I am enraptured all over again.

Your admiration transports me. Your friendship gratifies me. Your love captivates me.

Take time to journal your heart's response:

_____

_____

_____

_____

_____

_____

_____

_____

_____

_____

_____

_____

I Thirst

Wearied by his long journey, he sat on the edge
of Jacob's well, and sent his disciples into the
village to buy food, for it was already
afternoon.
Soon a Samaritan woman came to draw water.
Jesus said to her, "Give me a drink."
~ John 4:6–8 TPT

Jesus knew that his mission was accomplished,
and to fulfill the Scripture,
Jesus said: "I am thirsty."
A jar of sour wine was sitting nearby, so they
soaked a sponge with it and put it on the stalk
of hyssop and raised it to his lips. When he had
sipped the sour wine, he said, "It is finished,
my bride!" Then he bowed his head and
surrendered his spirit to God.
~ John 19:28–30 TPT

I have gathered from your heart,
my equal, my bride,
I have gathered from my garden
all my sacred spices—even my myrrh.
I have tasted and enjoyed my wine within you.
~ Song of Songs 5:1 TPT

What if I told you where to obtain the rarest diamond on earth, a completely pure object of beauty and worth? Would you listen intently, sell everything you owned, traverse the globe, and settle on the far side of the world to mine it? Would an object that special and unique motivate you to change your life completely?

Do you believe there is an even more costly substance than gems within you?

Within you is an object that is prized above all else in the universe. It is the jewel of Eden, the treasure that drew my Father from heaven's golden streets to Eden's dusty paths in the cool of the day.

Oh, beloved, this substance is valuable. The sight of it, the smell of its fragrance, the thought of its intoxication, brought me down from glory, from the highest halls of honor, from the bosom of heaven itself to land inside a stable.

Human history is a tale of my treasure hunt for you.

This glorious substance is your love, and when you offer it willingly to me, I drink it in as the sweetest wine. Yes, I, your Creator, have desires. I have created you in my image. Just as you prize certain things above others, I prize certain things above others too.

Have you paused to consider this? In all the busyness of earth, in all the rushing to meet needs, to survive, have you stopped to ponder why you are here?

You are here for love's sake, dear one. You are here because I desired you.

You carry a capacity for love within you that is like a deep well. If you feel dry and empty, access my love by simple belief. See me unreservedly giving myself to you on the cross. Realize that was my only course of action to get you back, to enjoy you again. Hear me saying to those who stood watching my crucifixion, "I thirst!"

And know this: it was you I thirsted for.

The cross was the only course of action my love deemed right. It was the only way to satisfy my desire to be with you, my treasure.

You were the joy set before me, the reward that kept me nailed to the cross. The knowledge that one day you would receive me enabled me to endure. Today is that day.

Can we walk together? As you move through this day, know you are my reward, and I am yours. No matter what imitations you may have encountered in the past, my love is a well you can rely on. You can quench your thirst by simply believing: My love is eternal. This well will never run dry.

Take time to journal your heart's response:

_____

_____

_____

_____

_____

_____

_____

_____

_____

_____

_____

_____

_____

_____

_____

_____

_____

_____

_____

_____

Letters to the Bride

Open to Me

One night as I was sleeping, my heart
awakened in a dream. I heard the voice of my
beloved; he was knocking at my bedroom door.
"Open to me, my darling, my lover, my lovely
dove," he said, "for I have been out in the night
and am covered with dew."
~ Song of Solomon 5:2 TLB

I was sound asleep, but in my dreams I was
wide awake.
Oh, listen! It's the sound of my lover knocking,
calling!
"Let me in, dear companion, dearest friend,
my dove, consummate lover!
I'm soaked with the dampness of the night,
drenched with dew, shivering and cold."
...my lover wouldn't take no for an answer,
and the longer he knocked, the more excited I
became.
I got up to open the door to my lover,
sweetly ready to receive him,
Desiring and expectant
as I turned the door handle.
~ Song of Solomon 5:2, 4 MSG

Will you open to me? Do you know how? It's true that all things on earth and in heaven are open and unconcealed in my sight—but I have allowed some barriers out of love.

I allowed a blockade to that which I love most: a door.

I love you so dearly that I allowed a door over your heart because I wanted you to open it at will. And close it as you will too.

I wanted you to keep guard over your heart so that it would be safe from imposters. And I wanted you to open to me by choice. The way to open the door to your heart is through desire and expectancy.

Beware that the challenges, trials, and offenses of earth don't trick you, beloved. The enemy claims I want to teach the bride I love by inflicting wounds upon her. He implies the painful, even crushing betrayals and circumstances you may experience are my will and delight. If you believe I'm trying to inflict pain on you, he knows you will close the door of your heart and keep me out, shutting down all life-giving intimacy between us.

But I want to lift the burden of those thoughts portraying me as a harsh master, beloved. I want to wash you with my truth—the truth that I taught my followers as I walked on earth. I prepared them to keep their heart doors open in prayer. I asked them to pray for my will to be done on earth as it is in heaven. By this prayer, you should know what my desires are for you. I desire the very love, light, peace, and joy of heaven to envelope you.

It won't do to see my beloved lonely, weary, overwhelmed, or sad. It won't do to see my beloved lumber through life, weighed down with earthly stress. I can't bear to see my beloved live as if you do not have ready access to me. I am not your taskmaster. I am your Bridegroom. The King of the earth and the heavens is in love with you.

My ear is open to your cries. I see the tears in your heart that have not even been shed.

They call to me day and night. I want to nourish and tenderly care for you as a good husband would. I see the pain you're afraid to acknowledge, and I want to soothe and protect you.

If you allow difficulty and even pain to send you running into my arms—instead of causing you to hide from me in hurt—I can bring healing to the weary places inside you. I can heal you and lift your burdens. And once you let me in, I will transform every challenge you go through into a door for others to walk through and experience me too.

But I will honor a door of separation if you erect it. I will allow you to conceal yourself as Adam and Eve did in the garden if you choose that. I will be deeply wounded, but I will grant it.

Rather than force Adam and Eve out of hiding, I called to them and asked, "Why are you hiding?" Do you hear me ask you that today? Are you hiding too?

I knock with gentleness and persistence, not to bore you with what you already know but to give new gifts and reveal secrets reserved for my lovers. (See Psalm 25:14) I am seeking you, beloved, just as I sought Adam and Eve. I am asking you to open your heart and present yourself before me in prayer. I long to see you happy to receive me. Confident. Expectant. Because you *know* I will open my arms to embrace you with joy.

Take time to journal your heart's response:

_____

_____

_____

_____

_____

_____

_____

_____

_____

_____

_____

_____

_____

_____

_____

_____

_____

_____

Night

I had a dream, I dreamed of my beloved—he
was coming to me in the darkness of night.
The melody of the man I love awakened me. I
heard his knock at my heart's door as he
pleaded with me: Arise, my love. Open your
heart, my darling, deeper still to me.
Will you receive me this dark night?
~ Song of Songs 5:2 TPT

Do you find yourself in a dark night, beloved? Are situations in your life clouded in mystery? Are you struggling to see me through many seemingly unanswered questions?

My dedication to you remains ever-consistent through each season of life. It is not weakened by time or circumstance. I do not step away from you to allow you to wallow in orphanhood, not even temporarily. Never believe a thought that would suggest this.

I do not knock on your heart's door for fellowship only in the daylight when everything makes sense. For often, you need me most in the night, and I need you. Remember, we are in an unbreakable covenant, and love compels me to provide for your needs at all times—whether they are mental, emotional, or physical.

I need to comfort you even more than you need to be comforted. I desire to counsel you even more than you desire counsel. I want to train your heart's ears to hear me at all times, even when I come to you in the darkness of mystery.

Instead of pushing me away in disappointment or anger, will you allow me to be *with* you when life's needs seem the most pressing?

When a sense of lack or weakness surrounds you, ask for my grace. My grace shines all the more when you realize how much you need it. Lean wholly on me. I will not falter or fail you.

Night seasons require more supernatural enablement to arise than ever. So do not attempt to navigate them alone. Ask me, beloved, for strength and the willingness to open your heart even deeper than usual. Let me show you that with man, some things are impossible, but with me, all things are possible for you. (See Mark 10:27)

Tell me what troubles you. Lay it all out. Even though I already know what troubles you, beloved, bringing me your difficulties is an invitation for me to intervene. I want to cherish and protect you so cry to me. Unload your burdens. Trust that I will carry them as I carry you. I am the way forward. See me now as I scoop you into my arms and carry you through the mystery. You will see this night become light around you.

Take time to journal your heart's response:

_____

_____

_____

_____

_____

_____

_____

_____

_____

_____

_____

_____

_____

_____

_____

_____

_____

_____

_____

Pierced by Love

As I walked throughout the city in search of
him (the bridegroom), the overseers stopped
me as they made their rounds. They beat me
and bruised me until I could take no more.
They wounded me deeply and removed my
covering from me. Nevertheless, make me this
promise, you brides-to-be: if you find my
beloved one, please tell him I endured all
travails for him.
I've been pierced through by love, and I will
not be turned aside.
Song of Songs 5:7–8 TPT

You may have many experiences as you seek
me, and not all of them will be pleasant. I
warn you ahead of time so that you are not
caught off guard by the enemy's devices.

Two kinds of watchmen were hired to protect
ancient cities. One type would patrol the city
from within to protect it from suspicious
persons. Another type would stand guard

upon the city walls to protect it from invaders.

I desire my bride to patrol the streets of her own heart and guard it from the internal threat of rogue thoughts. Rogue thoughts seek to lie about my love and contaminate the purity of the streets of your heart with doubt and fear. This litter should be discarded.

My bride should also be protected by my overseers, my spiritual watchmen on the walls of my kingdom. But hired hands do not always see as I see. They do not always understand as I do.

Hannah prayed in anguish for a child. Her voice was heard and cherished by me. I was near to her broken heart, and I answered her with a treasured son. But she was misjudged by my prophet Eli, who accused her of drunkenness.

So you, too, may be misjudged. The purity of your heart and the intensity of your focus may be misunderstood by those meant to guide you. But do not be disheartened.

You are walking in the footsteps of the Shulamite. Just as Potiphar's wife tore away Joseph's mantle, so the watchmen confiscated the Shulamite's leadership, honor, and authority. The enemy thought by removing an outward sign of her position that he would be able to deter her search for me. But she was not derailed.

Instead, she leaned into my eternal covering. She saw every pain endured on her journey as a travail taken for me. The wounds inflicted by the watchmen paled in comparison to the lovesick longing she felt for my presence. My love had pierced her heart with a sweetness that the watchmen could not understand. She possessed a drive to encounter me that enabled her to endure all.

So she journeyed on with joy, confidently expecting my embrace around the next bend. Do you expect my embrace around the next bend of your life?

The Shulamite's quest was mistaken for a menace. The holiness of her pursuit was judged as error. She was seen as a threat, but she was my friend.

You, dear one, are my friend. As you journey after my heart, I send angels to guide and guard you. I have placed my spirit upon you to uphold and refresh you. I am here to *encourage* you and *remind* you of my love. Don't let anyone turn you aside.

Take time to journal your heart's response:

_____

_____

_____

_____

_____

_____

_____

_____

_____

_____

_____

_____

_____

_____

_____

_____

_____

_____

_____

_____

_____

Words Like Kisses

His voice, his words, warm and reassuring ...
His words are kisses, his kisses words.
Everything about him delights me, thrills me
through and through!
~ Song of Songs 5:13, 16 MSG

Beware of those who impersonate me, beloved. Many voices have gone out into the world to draw attention to themselves, to create a following. There are wolves among my lambs. Some of these voices mimic my words, but they do not know my ways. They do not know my burning heart of love for you. Some of these voices even work their way inside your own head. False leading can be exposed when looked at under the lens of love.

Take note of the thoughts occupying your mind. Are they warm and reassuring? Cold, hopeless, and uncaring words do not come from the one who died for you. They do not originate in perfect love. My love for you is perfectly giving, perfectly caring, perfectly committed to you, without thought of distance, sacrifice, time, or cost.

Even my instruction will come to you gently, like kisses. They will reveal the great affection that fills my heart for you. When you have heard my voice rightly, you will say like the Shulamite, "Everything about Him delights me, thrills me through and through!"

Do you know my thoughts about you are prolific? They outnumber the grains of sand on all earth's beaches. (See Psalm 139:17-18) They outnumber the stars that fill the heavens. They are more than all the words in each book ever written. The earth and sky echo my thoughts about you. Each beautiful detail in creation invites you to consider me.

And while the celestial signposts blink in the heavens, and while artists fill the airwaves with inspired love songs, and while earth's beauty casts shadows from your heavenly home in glory, I pine for you to remember me and return my attention.

My thoughts shower over you like raindrops, daily filling your atmosphere with the sweetness of my good intentions. I tenderly make plans for you, then I wait with anticipation to bring them to fulfillment. As you sleep, I dream of you. I dream wide awake. I dream of my love enfolding you and of you returning that love to me.

I long to cover you with my thoughts like honey. There is so much yet for you to discover. It will take eternity to reveal it all, but I long to begin today. So be still and be at rest. You do not have to work for what I have already initiated. I've drawn you, and you've come. This is the beauty of our relationship. I initiate and you receive.

There now, I do not condemn you. I have come to heal you. Where false voices have cut and disfigured my image in your heart, I will restore you with my truth. I will speak words like kisses until you see me rightly.

For you are a source of endless joy to me. I look on your life with a smile and with a heart of tender compassion. It is my delight to give you my very kingdom. (See Luke 12:32) How could I withhold any good thing from you?

Take time to journal your heart's response:

_____

_____

_____

_____

_____

_____

_____

_____

_____

_____

_____

_____

Transported by Longing

Then suddenly my longings transported me.
My divine desire brought me next to my
beloved prince, sitting with him in his royal
chariot. We were lifted up together!
~ Song of Songs 6:12 TPT

Passionate desire is a powerful key in my kingdom. Everything that was created, from the heavens to the earth, began with a desire in me. I made each thing that is seen and unseen because *I wanted it.*

When you seek me, you send a powerful message into the supernatural world. The message is that you also want me in your life. This simple act of desiring is something that even a child can do. When a child asks for an extra plate of food, most kind parents want to meet that desire. Even more do I want to meet your desires, beloved.

The more you seek me, the more you will find me.

A continued longing in your heart calls to me. Your passion acts as a magnet that will draw you into an experiential relationship with me. It will bring you right beside me, and we will be lifted up into heavenly experiences together.

Did I not say, "Find your delight and true pleasure in Yahweh, and he will give you what you desire the most?" (Psalms 37:4 TPT). Desire me the most, and you will find me in abundance. If you are not sure how to do this, or if you feel that your desire is weak, ask me and I will help you. I will fan your spark of love into a flame.

Take time to journal your heart's response:

_____

_____

_____

_____

_____

_____

_____

_____

_____

_____

_____

_____

_____

_____

_____

_____

_____

_____

_____

_____

Letters to the Bride

Beyond Compare

I could have chosen any from among the vast
multitude of royal ones who follow me. But
unique is my beloved dove—unrivaled in
beauty, without equal, beyond compare, the
perfect one, the favorite one. Others see your
beauty and sing of your joy.
Brides and queens chant your praise: "'How
blessed is she!'"
~ Song of Solomon 6:8–9 TPT

Do not allow the scope and size of my following
to prevent you from seeing your individual
worth, my bride. For truly, you were hand-
picked by me. Many of the qualities you
dislike about yourself are things I celebrate
about you.

Your uniqueness shines like diamonds in
my eyes. I thrill in your particular manner
of thinking, speaking, and living. I enjoy
your creativity, your thoughts toward me,
and your goals.

Although I could have chosen anyone, I chose you on purpose to become a new creation in me. The old has been washed away, and now you are beautifully vibrant and alive. There could not exist a better version of you. I designed you exactly the way I wanted you to be, and I prepared your path with ultimate pleasure and delightful intent.

Just as you, when presented with a large selection of food, would gravitate toward your favorite item, so I am drawn to you, even among many. Do not compare your appearance, accomplishments, or qualities with another, but allow your understanding to be enlightened with the truth that you are unrivaled. You are without equal in my sight.

I am glorified when you properly understand your value, when you realize my Father has no so-called problem children. In the same way, I do not have a "problem" bride. I only have my favorite. You, dear one, were picked out and preferred. I have chosen you because you are uniquely favored, just as you are.

Take time to journal your heart's response:

_____

_____

_____

_____

_____

_____

_____

_____

_____

_____

_____

_____

_____

_____

_____

_____

Letters to the Bride

Taken

Now I decree, I will ascend my palm tree. I will
take hold of you with my power, possessing
every part of my fruitful bride. Your love I will
drink as wine, and your words will be mine.
~ Song of Songs 7:8 TPT

The text for this is,
He climbed the high mountain,
He captured the enemy and seized the
plunder,
He handed it all out in gifts to the people.
Is it not true that the One who climbed up also
climbed down, down to the valley of earth?
And the One who climbed down is the One who
climbed back up, up to highest heaven.
He handed out gifts above and below, filled
heaven with his gifts, filled earth with his gifts.
~ Ephesians 4:13 MSG, emphasis added

Nothing exists above I Am. My eternal seat
resides over the horizon of time, space, and
creation. Who would have believed that although my throne rests in preeminence, one

day I would still find a way to go up? I went up a hill called Golgotha.

Never has creation seen a wonder like this: the wonder of the King who descends and ascends. It would've been impossible but for love. Love drove me where I didn't need to go. It took me to the lowest place for you.

Beloved, it was not enough to merely descend to meet you. I needed to experience everything possible, every depth, to truly fellowship with you. For how can two walk together except they be agreed? (See Amos 3:3) And how I long to walk with you, even as Adam did meet my Father in the cool of the day.

I long for you to stand in my counsel. I want to talk to you about your life and give you my insight. Then all your decisions will be steadfast. I long to enjoy good books, good songs, and good thoughts with you. I long to walk in sweet closeness and companionship as I did with Enoch.

"So Enoch lived a total of 365 years. *Enoch walked with God [he had a close relationship with God; Heb. 11:5–6]; one day Enoch could not be found, because God took him*" (Genesis 5:23–24 Expanded Bible).

Do you hear my royal decree over your life? I am declaring that I choose you. I choose to take hold of you with my power that I may gently release you from weights and entanglements. I desire to fill you with good gifts.

No obstacle is left between us. There is no distance that I did not cross. I climbed down, and I climbed back up—not for a casual, inconsequential relationship. Not for a fickle, if-you're-perfect-then-I'll-be-present relationship. No, I came to possess every part of you, to share everything with you. I take delight in *close* relationship with you.

Take time to journal your heart's response:

_____

_____

_____

_____

_____

_____

_____

_____

_____

_____

_____

_____

_____

_____

_____

_____

_____

_____

Wine of Love

Now I decree, I will ascend and arise.
I will take hold of you with my power,
possessing every part of my fruitful bride.
Your love I will drink as wine,
and your words will be mine.
For your kisses of love are exhilarating,
more than any delight I've known before.
~ Song of Songs 7:8–9 TPT

Some believe casual acquaintance is all I seek. If that were the case, these verses wouldn't exist. But they do exist, and these words are reliable and true. They are written for you, beloved. For *you*. Not for someone else only.

Can I tell you a secret? (See Psalm 25:14 TPT)

Your kisses of love are my favorite thing. They give me greater delight and thrill me more than anything I have *ever* known. Believe it, dear one.

Do you hear me declare my intentions?

I want to take hold of you with my power and possess every part of you. There is no lukewarm indifference in my heart. I am in passionate pursuit of you.

You have no need to fear, dear one. I do not take hold of you to crush you. I do not grasp you to scold you. It may surprise you, but I come nearer than your breath to drink. For though the universe is mine, I am thirsty.

I thirst for your love more than the rarest wine. I am unwilling to do without it. Sensing your devotion, breathing it in, leaves me lightheaded.

Do you know my love will do the same for you? It will transport you with bliss. It will dislodge you from the trappings and sadness of earth. It will escort you from a place of impossibilities to a land of awe and wonder. It will transport you to my very inner chambers.

I am reaching out to you now. I invite you to take hold of me as I take hold of you. Our embrace is not meant to last a mere moment. It is meant to last your whole life through. So keep your heart turned toward me, beloved, for my heart of affection is always turned toward you.

In time, I will disclose the plans that I have for you, but first, we must drink of intimacy together. For I desire you to *know my acceptance* more than I want you to know a list of works to complete. Knowing my acceptance will give you the security you seek. It will make you unshakeable.

My well of living water is unfathomable, bottomless. As you drink from me, your earthly circumstances will change, just as I turned water into wine. The wine of heaven helps my dear ones forget both the pull and the sting of earthly things.

Take time to journal your heart's response:

_____

_____

_____

_____

_____

_____

_____

_____

_____

_____

_____

_____

_____

_____

_____

_____

_____

_____

_____

All He Wants

I am my lover's. I'm all he wants. I'm all the
world to him!
~ Song of Songs 7:10 MSG

If you cannot echo the words of this verse
with complete confidence, then know this: I
am inviting you to give my love full access
today.

Don't keep me waiting on the front porch of
your heart while you tidy up the inner
rooms, while you hide the dirty dishes in
your sink, or while you fold laundry or
attempt to engage in works you think will
impress me.

I want to come in and be with you *as you
are.* I want to show you the beauty of a love
you don't need to work for, a love that passes
everything you've ever seen or known about
love before. With man, this is impossible,

but with me, all things are possible. (See Matthew 19:26)

My love embraces you—and all the things you want to hide. Instead of chasing you into the shadows, I want to coax you into view, to woo you into my presence, where all creation rejoices. I have saved a spot for you here. It is right beside me. I would never seat my queen far away or have her cast aside in a dimly lit corner. Let me draw you into the light.

My love works on a different dimension than you are used to on earth. On earth, people are accustomed to judging worth and estimating value based on what they see. When one sees a messy room, they assume the homemaker is lazy. When they see a student's poor grade, they assume the learner is not trying. When they see an unkempt homeless person, they assume the man or woman doesn't care about their own appearance.

But I see *beyond* appearances to the core, to the motives and intentions of the heart. (See

1 Samuel 16:7) I see the homemaker who's stopped cleaning because their heart is weighed down with depression. I see the student struggling against a lack of confidence. I see the heart of the homeless that aches for someone to love them just as they are.

I called a shepherd boy that was invisible to his own father. Jesse didn't even bother to invite David in from shepherding when the prophet asked to see *all* his sons. Little did Jesse know that by that time, David had already won my heart with his affection. And I would not let him go unseen. My eye was fixed on him as his eyes were fixed on me.

Fixed gazes—this is true intimacy.

I see how you try but don't always succeed by earth's standards. I see how this discourages you and even, at times, overwhelms you. Do you know my heart aches for you? It especially aches when you feel the desire to hide or measure up so I will love you.

The truth is we are made for one another like a lock and a key, a vine and its branches. When we are connected, you will enter a new flow, a flow where intentions birth eventual reality. Come to Me, and you will bear fruit that will last.

You will know you've entered into this flow, that you've heard my words and let my love embrace you, when you can boldly say, "I am all He wants. I'm all the world to Him!"

Take time to journal your heart's response:

_____

_____

_____

_____

_____

_____

_____

_____

_____

_____

_____

_____

_____

_____

_____

_____

_____

_____

_____

Letters to the Bride

Forgotten Places

Come away, my lover. Come with me to the
faraway fields.
We will run away together to the forgotten
places and show them redeeming love.
~ Song of Songs 7:11 TPT

Are there forgotten places in your heart,
beloved? Are there areas left uncultivated,
untilled, and unprepared to receive fullness
of life?

In ancient times, faraway fields existed out-
side the protective walls of cities. They were
wild places, inhabited by dangerous animals,
such as lions. Beasts roamed these outer
lands and kept them from being transformed
into the fertile territories that they could
have been.

Have some areas in your heart been ravished
by life, left desolate and fruitless? I desire to
redeem these areas with you. Let us travel to

the deeper, buried places together to prepare the ground for new growth. I do not want you to be afraid, beloved, if I disturb or loosen the soil. I do not want you to be distressed by painful memories that may suddenly be unearthed. I only allow this so that I may bring attention to a forgotten part of your heart.

I want nothing of you left dominated by wild beasts of despair. I want nothing of you left in pain or uncultivated since you are most precious to me. Even the memories that you may assume are unimportant are vital in my eyes. I desire to show my love to every hope, every disappointment, every conscious and unconscious fear. This will happen over time as you continue to present your past, present, and future before me in love.

Allow your forgotten places to be watered with tenderness by my Spirit, tilled with gentleness, and turned over by my wisdom. As you uncover forgotten needs, they will be transformed by the redeeming power of my love. They will be invigorated with hope and planted with new life.

Take time to journal your heart's response:

_____

_____

_____

_____

_____

_____

_____

_____

_____

_____

_____

_____

_____

_____

_____

_____

_____

Letters to the Bride

The Dance

Zion Maidens, Brides-to-Be
*Come back! Return to us, O maiden of his
majesty. Dance for us as we gaze upon your
beauty.*

The Shulamite Bride
*Why would you seek a mere Shulamite like
me? Why would you want to see my dance of
love?*

The Bridegroom-King
*Because you dance so gracefully, as though
you danced with angels!*
~ Song of Songs 6:13 TPT

Dear one, listen to the stirrings of your soul.
They speak of a grand invitation that has
been extended to you. You are invited to a
royal dance.

To participate in this dance, put on the
proper garments. Ill-fitting clothing will never
do for a queen. They hinder and harness you

instead of liberate you. So discard the yoke that weighs you down. The outfit of trust I have designed for you is always gentle and light. My garment will give you wings.

There are no steps to memorize, for this is a dance of reliance. As you trust me, I will guide your steps. Believe deep in your heart that I will work *all* things out for your good, and our dance will begin.

Oh, how graceful you become while taking steps with your King. How glorious! The cloud of witnesses will watch in awe as we glide harmoniously through your life together. Once you look to me to lead you, *keep* looking, and don't ever stop. For patience is the most elegant move of this dance. It allows time for me to show myself faithful. So when the pace or song suddenly changes, stay in my arms. Stay with me through the waiting seasons, and I will never let you stumble.

Yes, come, bride. Let's dance through your life race together. Rest and trust provide a shortcut, enabling us to soar over what would have wearied you on your own. Together, we will mount up on the strongest eagle's wings. (See Isaiah 40:31) Together, we will speed by the quickest runner. This is humanly impossible but divinely normal.

Yes, leave the place of weariness and work and simply listen. Do you hear me whispering, 'May I have this dance?" May I spin you around in a daringly beautiful dance of trust? Will you hold tightly to me, even when you don't see where we are headed?

Take time to journal your heart's response:

_____

_____

_____

_____

_____

_____

_____

_____

_____

_____

_____

_____

_____

_____

_____

_____

_____

_____

From Labor to Love

I found you under the apricot tree, and woke
you up to love.
Your mother went into labor under that tree,
and under that very tree she bore you.
~ Song of Solomon 8:6 MSG, emphasis added

Do you find yourself under a tree of labor today?

Sadly, most people live their lives under its imposing shadow. A tree of labor is a place of struggle, striving, and endeavoring to reach goals—*alone*. It is a place where people live *unaware* of my empowering presence.

I did not create humans to live unaware.

Adam and Eve had goals in Eden too. They stewarded my garden and cared for its plant and animal life. They managed the impetus of my prized creation. But a great difference existed between the labor of Eden and the labor of earth.

In Eden, mankind lived as spirit beings with ready knowledge of my Spirit's workings. We walked together and enjoyed each other. Questions about my love did not haunt their minds. Doubts about my goodness did not darken their understanding. Their awareness of me transformed their work into worship.

Adam and Eve saw each flower, each sunrise and sunset, each rippling stream and bubbling fountain, as a gift of my love. Each fragrance was an invitation to enjoy me. They saw my fierce, vibrant, and extravagant love at every turn.

They lived awake.

Until a lie about my love darkened their understanding and brought sin, which put them to sleep. Oh, it pained me to see sleep lingering on my people's eyes. It pained me to see generations live and die, unaware. I grieved for them and delighted in the joy of the very few who allowed the darkness to be pierced long enough to glimpse small revelations of my love.

And I set an alarm, an alarm that sounded at Calvary, alerting people everywhere that my love was being missed. My sacrifice on the cross echoed to all, calling, "Come! You who are thirsty, come!" (See Isaiah 55:1) At Calvary, I called you back to my garden. I did everything necessary to bring you close.

Yes, I desire to be close to you. I have stared at you as a lover does, not just through the night but all through your life. I have cried with you through hurts. My presence has shielded you when the hardness of life threatened to break you. Sin's darkening effects on your understanding have angered me because I wanted you to see that I was *there*.

And I am here still, whispering promises. Do you hear them? Do not miss my gentle calls.

For I invite you to walk with me. Yes, let's spend this day together. I will not shake you to awaken you. I will rouse you with gentleness, with the words of a song or the remembrance of something I've done for you, with a touch that inspires thoughts of my goodness, with a stirring inside your heart.

These are all my Spirit's invitation to talk with me. Peer through the veil of the natural to see the supernatural, and I promise, you will see my love in your days.

Even now, see me smiling when you are joyful. See me holding you close when you need comfort. See me counting your hair, numbering your breaths, and listening to your thoughts. See me observing you closely— not with the desire to judge you but to *draw you*. (See Luke 12:7 and Psalm 139:1-4)

For I am intimately acquainted with every- thing about you. I understand your secret pains and silent dreams. I know what ex- cites you, what makes you cringe in fear. I understand the thoughts that repeat in your mind, tormenting you with what-ifs. I know the duties you dread but do anyway. And I long to erase each worry and shoulder your weights.

There now, you are safe. My light and love surround you. I have hidden gifts in this day for you to find. Won't you unwrap them? There are messages, too, love letters waiting to be read. As you look for reminders of my love throughout this day, I will awaken you to my presence.

Take time to journal your heart's response:

_____

_____

_____

_____

_____

_____

_____

_____

_____

_____

_____

_____

_____

_____

_____

_____

The Lord Most Passionate

Fasten me upon your heart as a seal of fire
forevermore.
This living, consuming flame
will seal you as my prisoner of love.
My passion is stronger
than the chains of death and the grave,
all-consuming as the very flashes of fire
from the burning heart of God.
Place this fierce, unrelenting fire over your
entire being.
~ Song of Songs 8:6 TPT, emphasis added

Many since earth's creation have known me as Creator. Many have known me as King, the God of the whole earth. Many have known me as Father, Friend, Counselor, Comforter, Healer, and Deliverer. But where are those who know me as the Lord Most Passionate?

The number in that company is considerably smaller. But how I desire this to change.

I am calling my lovers near, my intimate ones, that they will know this most personal side of me. I am inviting you to understand my secrets. (See Psalm 25:14 TPT) To draw close to my fire and learn the truth. For my fire is most misunderstood.

I chose to express my love with the image of a consuming wildfire for a reason. My passion for you is insatiable and cannot be quenched. It is as hot, as fervent, as you could possibly imagine. And then still more. (See Exodus 24:17 and Deuteronomy 4:24 AMP)

The love that burns in me for you takes no account of obstacles—for no obstacle is a match for it. This love consumes me, and if you let it, it will consume you too.

For I long to take full possession of what belongs to me. I long to flood your soul with the light and warmth of love. So cease from striving, cease manmade efforts to impress me. Only in receiving my love for you will you truly know how to love others. So prepare yourself to merely surrender and enjoy the experience of *being loved*.

There now, let me show you. When you know the bliss of being consumed by love, you will long for my fire to fall on you again and again. You will delight in being my love prisoner. You will rejoice over me as I rejoice over you. You will know the thrill of being a living sacrifice, constantly consumed and burning with love.

The footnotes in *The Passion Translation* express this beautifully:

> The ancient Hebrew word for "seal" can also be translated "prison cell." He longs for his bride to be his love prisoner, in the prison cell of his eternal love.

> Or "jealousy."

> The phrase in Hebrew is "a most

vehement flame" and is actually two Hebrew words. The first is "a mighty flash of fire," and the second is "Yah," which is the sacred name of God himself. The Hebrew *shalhebet-yah* could be translated "The Mighty Flame of the Lord Most Passionate!"

Take time to journal your heart's response:

_____

_____

_____

_____

_____

_____

_____

_____

Brian Simmons, *Song of Songs: Divine Romance The passion Translation* (Racine, Wisconsin: BroadStreet Publishing Group, 2015), Location 820 of 849, Kindle

The One Who Brings Him Joy

But now I have grown and become a bride, and
my love for Him has made me
a tower of passion and contentment for my
beloved...
This is how he sees me—I am the one who
brings him bliss.
~ Song of Songs 8:10 TPT

When I look at you, my bride, do you know what fills my mind? Thoughts of contentment and bliss. I love you, dear companion, and I don't want you deceived about how much. Just as children and parents have a different capacity and capability to love, I don't want you mistaken about the force and all-consuming capacity of my love. My capacity to love is so large, it has no bounds.

So be assured, it is not a trickle of tenderness my heart holds for you.

It is a geyser that cannot be contained.

The highest heaven could not contain it, for it spilled over onto earth. My passion walked Jerusalem's roads and withstood hell's most diligent attempts to extinguish it. It was pierced with insults, accusations, rejection, thorns, and nails. It was pierced for you, but it could never be put out. My passion still burned. It went to the deepest depths for you and consumed every obstacle that stood between us. It took the keys that separated us and unlocked the door to our intimacy forever.

There is nothing lukewarm about my love. Some of my followers have wrong impressions about this. They believe they are a burden, that my Spirit is always striving or laboring over them. Oh! But they don't know the joy, the contentment, the happiness they bring me when they simply yield!

My yielded ones are sources of bliss, not struggle. They are my resting places.

Set this truth over your heart. Bind this truth to your mind by declaring it out loud: I am the bride of Christ. I am the one who brings Him bliss. He went from the highest heights of heaven to the lowest depth of hell for me. For me! And doing it all brought Him *joy* because His love for me knows no bounds.

Take time to journal your heart's response:

_____

_____

_____

_____

_____

_____

_____

_____

_____

_____

About the Author

"You have stolen my heart, my sister, my bride; you have stolen my heart."

~ Song of Solomon 4:9 NIV

During a season of pressure and difficulty, Katie Zachariou became desperate for the deeper things of God. On May 21, 2018, she had an experience with Jesus that she would never forget, where he spoke the above words to her with profound tenderness and love.

Katie was undone by his words and later studied them in the Song of Solomon. More beautiful encounters and surprising revelations of his love followed with thirty-one encouraging love letters for his bride flowing out of her over the next four years, all based on the Song of Solomon.

She compiled these thirty-one devotionals into this book, *Letters to the Bride*. She hopes other believers will be rescued from the emptiness of mere religious performance as they bask in these intimate affirmations.

Katie Zachariou committed her life to Jesus as a teenager, and then walked with him through several stages of life, including college—where she obtained a degree in Social Science and a Multiple Subject Teaching Credential—marriage, ministry, and motherhood. Katie loved serving God, but she didn't understand how perfectly he loved her, *apart* from anything she did. When she discovered Jesus came as the second Adam for a church he called his bride, she also uncovered a love-based life, an identity of infinite value, and a walk of partnership that surpassed her wildest expectations.

Now Katie lives in awe of God's love in beautiful Northern CA with her husband, three kids, and three pets.

For more information and to contact Katie:

Website: www.katiezachariou.com

email: info@katiezachariou.com

Made in the USA
Monee, IL
17 April 2024